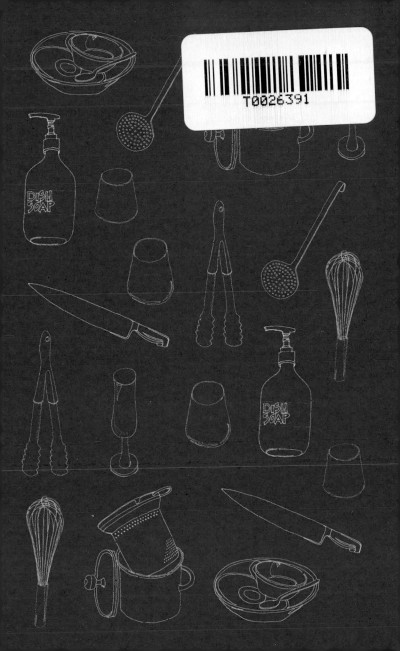

T0026391

HOW TO

Wash the Dishes

———

Peter Miller

Illustrated by Colleen Miller

ROOST BOOKS

ROOST BOOKS
An imprint of Shambhala Publications, Inc.
2129 13th Street
Boulder, Colorado 80302
roostbooks.com

9 8 7 6 5 4 3

Printed in China

⊗ This edition is printed on acid-free paper that meets the
American National Standards Institute Z39.48 Standard.
✿ Shambhala Publications makes every effort to print on recycled paper.
For more information please visit www.shambhala.com.

Roost Books is distributed worldwide by Penguin Random House, Inc.,
and its subsidiaries.

Designed by CAT GRISHAVER
Illustrations by COLLEEN MILLER

Library of Congress Cataloging-in-Publication Data
Names: Miller, Peter, 1946– author. | Miller, Colleen, illustrator.
Title: How to wash the dishes / Peter Miller; illustrated by Colleen Miller.
Description: First edition | Boulder: Roost, 2020.
Identifiers: LCCN 2019022895 | ISBN 9781611807622 (paperback)
Subjects: LCSH: Home economics—Humor. | Dishwashing—Humor.
Classification: LCC TX295 .M49 2020 | DDC 648—dc23
LC record available at http://lccn.loc.gov/2019022895

A DEDICATION

———————

It is always my hope, and the hope of many people, the hope of every civilization, that we share our lives. We eat together and, with luck, we realize what fortune that is. We do the dishes. As simple as that.

YOU DO NOT NEED A BOOK TO TELL YOU
HOW TO WASH THE DISHES.

And yet . . .

If you avoid looking at the sink, dreading what you might find there, this book will help.

If the sink is piled high, in a chaotic, pick-up sticks sculpture of unwashed equipment, knives, dishes, and glasses, this book will help.

If you are a guest at a friend's home and notice that the dishwasher is full to its brim—*before* dinner—this book will help.

If you sincerely want to enjoy your time in the kitchen, this book will be invaluable.

———

Asking yourself,

What am I doing?

will help you overcome

the habit of wanting

to complete things quickly.

Smile to yourself and say,

Washing this dish is

the most important job in my life.

When you are really there,

washing the dishes can be

a deep and enjoyable experience.

But if you wash them

while thinking about other things,

you are wasting your time,

and probably not

washing the dishes well

either.

—THICH NHAT HANH,

The Heart of the Buddha's Teaching

Contents

———

HOW TO

Wash the Dishes

———

1

A PRIMER FOR
Washing the Dishes

———

ALMOST EVERYONE, at some point in their life, washes the dishes. Not many will do it well and even fewer will look forward to it.

It is a curious task, washing the dishes. Some people save it for themselves, some do it as a sacrifice, and some dread it or avoid doing it entirely.

Washing the dishes in a sink, with clean, warm water, is a luxury. If you have ever lived without clean running water or warm water, or even if you have ever camped in the wilderness, you already know this. It is also a task of order and of health and hygiene. The kitchen is an operating room, and although you may not always be the one operating, you are the one cleaning up after a kind of surgery. You have all the surfaces and all the equipment to scrub and make ready for the next use. You may be lucky enough to have a dishwasher. There will be a mention of dishwashers here and there, but this is a book about washing the dishes, not about machines that wash dishes. This is a book about enjoying your time and using it well. The dishwasher is the express train; your kitchen sink is the local.

This is a primer for the task, with rules and regulations, safety and sense, and a start and a finish. When the kitchen lights are dimmed, there should be a dish towel and a bowl drying. You have finished the meal and closed up shop.

The Task

A task is generally easier if you are prepared and have some plans and some knowledge about the job ahead. Here is a list of the elements.

- Clean all the dishes, pots and pans, glasses, silverware, containers, and surfaces, including the stove, walls, counters, and burners.

- Waste neither water nor soap, being both accurate and economical.

- Work safely in regard to yourself and other people who may be helping.

- Protect the equipment: care for the knives, pans, mixers, strainers, and such so they stay sharp, rust-free, and ready for their next appearance.

- Safeguard the food: store leftovers and staples wisely and correctly, especially with regard to bacteria and shelf life.

- Leave the kitchen bright, fresh, and ready for the next meal—as if it was new, and you had not been there.

Basic Tools

There are only a few things you need to wash the dishes well. You may already have them. You might also check that they have not been worked to a nub and want replacing. There are times that it is a treat to get a new sponge, scrubber, or dishtowel.

TO START

You will need a container for the dishwater. It can be a dishpan or even a rubber, plastic, or stainless bowl, and it should take up no more than three-quarters of the sink; you will need room to work and to rinse.

You will also need:
A good sponge or dishcloth
A good scrubber
A good dish soap
Several fresh, dry dish towels

When the dishes are washed, you will need a drying rack or an empty dishwasher to stack them.

The bowl is your tractor, your plow, and your very best piece of equipment.

At the Center of It All

Your bowl of soap and water is the center of your dish-washing operation. Everything depends upon it. The economy of doing the dishes is directly affected by it. If you protect your hot soapy water, you will use less detergent, your surfaces will be cleaner, and your glasses and dishware will be brighter. The bowl is your tractor, your plow, and your very best piece of equipment.

You may fill your bowl six to eight times during a clean-up if there are multiple dishes. When you fill it, do it slowly. As it is filling the first time, you can wash all the stuff on the periphery: the lids, the loose glassware, and the serving spoons. If you let the hot water run slowly, you may well have time to clear your counters of the stray bits and pieces that are generated by cooking. Clean and open space is your most intimate ally.

I usually use a thin, five-quart stainless-steel bowl for doing the dishes. It is a little battered and does other duty as a salad bowl or quick tossing bowl, but its main work is in the sink. It is not high sided, as I do not want it to be big enough to hide a sharp, eight-inch knife. I do not need a great depth of soapy water; I need its strength much more than its volume.

The soap bowl must not be so big that it clogs the sink. You need to be able to get in there, to clear food waste, to rinse silverware, to clear sponges and dishcloths, to rinse your hands. There are even times you will be best served by lifting the soap bowl out of the sink and putting it aside until bigger issues are resolved.

If you ever go camping and must cook for several people, you will learn a great deal about soapy water. It takes time to get the water to boil, so once you have added the detergent, you must protect the water, or you will have to refill your bowl numerous times and will be at the task for hours.

For some reason, some people imagine that it is sensible to pour the last of their milky coffee into the bowl of soapy water or to slide a half-clean plate into it. The truth is, the water must be kept as far as possible from food or grease or other liquids. They dilute its strength. You will use it as your center of operations, so defend it. When the pan with duck grease arrives, get your soapy water to safety!

When the pan
with duck grease
arrives, get
your soapy water
to safety!

Rinsing

Rinse everything first, before it goes into your dish-water, before it is stacked for washing. Unrinsed dinner plates or salad dressing or gravy destroys the strength and abilities of the whole bowl of soap and water. A stack of plates that has been rinsed takes half the labor of a stack of plates that still has food on them.

The rinsing allows you to prioritize the dishes, pots, pans, and such. It will also keep you mobile and able to adjust to what is coming. For example, the arrival of an oven pan that was used to roast a chicken and then was heated anew on the stovetop to make gravy will affect everything. If you leave the pan in the sink, then all of the other dishes will take on its grease or at least have to tiptoe around the greasy, sprawling new arrival. Clean it first, or park it well away from your workspace with some soap of its own. It can wait.

The Dishwashing Sequence

Here is a tried-and-true method for washing dishes:

1. Rinse the dishes, glasses, silverware, and pans as they come in.

2. Use the good soapy water to help by scooping some from the bowl onto a sponge or dishcloth.

3. If there is a lot of silverware, grab a smaller bowl, rinse the pieces under running water and add them to that bowl with a squirt of detergent. Set it aside and let it sit.

4. If the pans cannot be easily rinsed, and the stains are tough, rinse what you can and then fill them with water, add some detergent, and let them soak.

5. Keep the dirty dishes on one side of your counter, the rinsed on another. Do not let dirty dishes traipse all over the place like muddy shoes.

6. It is sensible and helpful to wash the dishes in the order of their weight. Start with the glasses, move to the smaller plates and cups, then on to the larger plates, platters, and smaller pans. When they are washed and cleared, finish with the cooking equipment, starting first with the smaller pieces and ending with the bulkiest. Let soak what needs to soak.

7. If you mix washing glassware with pans or platters, you risk breaking the lighter, more fragile pieces. As well, when you are washing a glass, you are more careful and gentler than you need to be with a greasy sauté pan. Keep them apart and distinct, for the techniques to wash them are apart and distinct.

8. To wash the glasses, use the freshest, soapiest water and dip into it with the dishcloth, so you can clean both the inside and outside of the glass.

9. To wash the plates, make certain there is room for them. They each take up a square foot of space once they get unstacked. Get them cleaned with your dishcloth and into a rack or a dishwasher.

10. To wash the bigger pots and pans, be careful that the glasses and other smaller pieces are resolved and out of the way. You are on to harder surfaces, which require a little more elbow grease and usually more soaping and rinsing. It is a contest of individual pieces—their handles and lids and interiors.

11. Return to your bowl of soapy water. If it becomes diluted, pour some of what is left into pots and pans waiting to get cleaned and throw the rest away. Start over, with fresh water and fresh detergent. There is always a kind of rush to doing dishes, and if there is music playing in the background, it is always the time for a faster beat. But do add the water slowly—so much can get done while the bowl is refilling.

Ecology, Economy, and Order

Do not waste water or soap. Water is life. It is precious, and if you are lucky enough to have it come easily out of your faucet, treat it with gratitude and respect. Review your water footprint. Every time you wash dishes is an opportunity to practice mindfulness and to reduce waste.

It is an ecology, washing dishes, with boundaries and cautions and results. As you pay attention to the details, so shall your work show the advantages. You are, in a way, running an airport, and there are many planes that need attention: some are waiting to land, some are overloaded, some need to be cleaned and serviced, and others need to take off. You have runways heading in multiple directions, and they all need to remain fluid and accurate. The sink and the bowl are your control tower. There will be times of some crisis, and it is your task to find the ways through and to keep the system up to speed and functioning efficiently. The order will protect against accidents.

Soaps

There are many dish soaps. Some were created long before any ecological issues were around to influence their composition. Some have been adjusted accordingly; some have simply been scented. And some soap companies have spent more money on advertising than on their product itself.

Find a soap that works best for you and is free of chemicals and preservatives that can be harmful to the environment when they go down the drain. Find one that cleans grease, brightens glassware, and is kind to your skin, your plumbing, and the Earth. This is something you will use every day, so it is worth having one you feel good about.

SOAP DECANTING

There are many forms of dish soap, including liquid, crystal, and powder. Whatever the form, it often sits prominently on your counter. If you use a liquid soap, consider decanting it. Liquid soap containers are typically littered with words and color, since part of their task is to sell themselves to you from the crowded shelves at the grocery store. But when you are washing the dishes, the goal is to just enjoy washing the dishes. You do not need to be sold anything or convinced of anything. Consider decanting the soap into something that has no words or graphics. This will take some of the visual clutter off your counter and also allow you to buy the soap in bulk and just refill the container, creating less waste, saving money, and giving yourself a space to wash, free of advertisement and clutter.

Find a vessel that you like. Choose a clear glass one perhaps, with a cork stopper, so you will be able to see how much soap you have left. And you will know, immediately, that it is the dish soap. You will also be more conscious of keeping the vessel itself clean.

Sponges

Uncolored, natural, pop-up sponges, made from all-natural cellulose have better absorbency, better texture, and a better smell than the nylon versions. Since they are a natural product, they need a little extra care. For one, you must rinse them completely at the end of doing dishes. If there is soap left in them, they can tend to sour. And the sour smell is not at all what you want. But if you tend to them—rinsing them with cold water, ringing them out well—they will last, and they will serve perfectly.

Store them so they can dry, ensuring their surface is not touching a damp counter or such. If you do not have a perforated shelf, you can always leave them to dry on top of a small, upright glass. On occasion these sponges can be difficult to find, but keep looking and ask your local shop to keep them on hand.

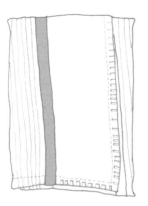

Dishcloths

Another wonderful tool to accompany your sponge is a dishcloth. It is like a sponge, but it is more intimate and precise and can do the best work on silverware and glasses. I will never be without one, now. My daughter lives in Sweden, where dishcloths are ubiquitous, and she brings them back as presents. They brighten the grittiest part of the kitchen workroom.

It is the dishcloth that best cleans the stove and the knobs and the backsplash. It holds soap, it covers a good area, and it rinses perfectly. With the dishcloth, you can feel if there is any grit left on knives or pans or spatulas, and because they let you be more precise than a sponge, they can clean deeply into the corners of your sink.

While I use a sponge to clean the outside of pans, the bottoms of dishes, and the surface of platters, I use a dishcloth in tighter spots like the corners and crannies of colanders and mixers and equipment. The dishcloth is also valuable for wiping the counters. It absorbs well, is easily rinsed, and will not retain odors or colors.

If you used a dish towel to wipe the counters, then that dish towel would be of no further use for that meal. It must be fully cleaned and dried. But the dishcloth, by virtue of its material and weave, rinses completely and dries quickly. It can get right back to task.

Dish Towels

You will need dish towels. Some people have very strong opinions about the dish towel, as some people do about everything. Some will say it needs to be at least part linen while others say it should be all cotton, contain no cotton, or be quilted. The world has many variations, and I have found a few things to be true.

The Danes, the Swedes, and the Finns love their dish towels and have done enormous research on the features that make the best ones. Weave and the quality of cotton and terry cloth are especially considered. They have many versions of the dish towel, all of which dry and absorb well and also add color and grace to a kitchen. Scandinavia is famous for long, dark winters, so they are very conscious of the advantages of color and of getting things perfectly dry.

The French consider their dish towels to be so superb and in such demand that they may wonder why there are even any others. You can buy them at flea markets, department stores, even design stores, and you can choose them by their feel or texture. Many kitchens in France have drawers filled with cotton dish towels, some having been used for generations.

Twenty years ago, we were visited by an agent for an Italian fabric company who was hoping to sell their products in Seattle and the Northwest. Nothing came of it, but we were able to place one order for napkins, placemats, and dish towels. To this day, I can tell you precisely what those towels look and feel like, and only on special occasions do we use the napkins. They are, in my mind, the most elegant that I have ever used.

QUALITIES OF A GOOD DISH TOWEL

You do not need a dish towel simply to finish washing the dishes. That is only a curtain call to its day. Its real work begins at the very start of cooking and continues right through to dish drying, keeping the runways clear, the tools at the ready, and the loose ends put away.

A good dish towel must do several things well. It must absorb water when you are drying and be efficient enough to handle several large pans. It must be large enough and thick enough to double as a potholder. It must be wash-able and clean well, and it must dry quickly. You can use a dish towel to dry fish and chicken, but you must remember to throw it in the wash immediately afterward.

Find a dish towel that you love the look and feel of. It is, in a way, both a scarf and a tool for a working kitchen, bringing pattern and color but also working as hard as any sauté pan. A dish towel must skirt the open flames, protect your hand from being burned, and take the moisture from the most delicate glasses, all in the same meal. It works as hard as all of the other tools and dishes, yet it is the only one that gets dressed up.

Find a dish towel that you love the look and feel of. It is, in a way, both a scarf and a tool for a working kitchen, bringing pattern and color but also working as hard as any sauté pan.

STORING AND CARING FOR YOUR TOWELS

We keep separate piles of towels. In one drawer are the working towels, distinguished either by their cooking scars or their simple design. They can do any task from acting as a flame retardant to cleaning up spilled grease and bloody counters. In a separate drawer, we keep the hand-selected towels. They could do any task, as well, but they have more intricate patterns and a finer texture. We have purchased them all over the world or received them as gifts, and each one typically has a story behind it. We use these towels only to dry or to serve.

With any dish towel, you must have a system to keep it dry. Towel bars work well, and hooks are okay. We use a Swedish kitchen hook that clamps the towel and then releases it as you reach for it. The towel must be able to dry. A wet, even damp, towel is not only less effective, it literally conducts heat, so if you use one to reach for a hot pan, it is in some ways worse than using your bare hand.

There is also the issue of keeping the towels clean. If you are rigorous about their storage and their regular washing, then it should not be an issue. You may want to keep the two types of dish towels separate. The harder working versions will have food or stains on them and might require a different degree of soaking and fabric washing.

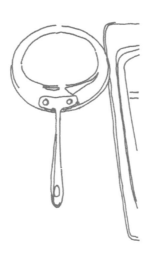

Cleaning Tools between Uses

Prepping takes bowls and tools and cutting boards, and they all need to be kept moving. Each piece, each bowl or board, may be a part of other elements of a dinner, so as it finishes one task, it must be readied to help with another.

When you soak the broccoli, remember that the bowl will only need a very quick wash to be ready for the next assignment. But be sure to use hot water and soap as the broccoli can be a little greasy and even a little wormy. Then rinse it well and use a dish towel to dry it. The bowl is your responsibility. You know where it has been, what it has done, and what it will take for it to be ready for the next task. It is yours to keep track of, and yours to make ready.

One of the bowls may have been used for a salad, and that poses a different task. You need to rinse that bowl well, and you need to do the rinsing away from everything else, or the oily film from the dressing will get on everything, every glass and saucer. Always check quickly to see if the salad bowl could do a second duty before you wash it. The leftover dressing is very good with bits of vegetables or cut-up meats or sautéed kale or croutons. Once these bits have soaked up the rest of the dressing, then wash the bowl.

To wash the salad bowl, clear the sink, rinse the bowl in hot water, and immediately get some soap into it to break up the oil. Finish cleaning the bowl thoroughly, or the salad dressing will trail you everywhere. When you dry it, check to make certain the surface has no film left on it.

I have several skimmers, three or four tongs, two ladles, and a dozen wooden and rubber spoons, each with its own qualities. If I use one for the peas, I will need it soon for the asparagus, and so forth. You can only manage the parts if you can quickly, thoroughly, and easily clean each one right after use.

A spoon or spatula may be going from a strong smell to a light one, from garlic to a sauce that must not have a hint of garlic, or it may be heading into hot oil and so must be dry or the spatter would be terrible. You can only control these things with a fresh bucket of soapy water and supply of dish towels.

Never put any tools in the dishwasher. They need to be at the ready. Wash them, dry them, and have them in place for the next task.

The View from a Sink

I recall many sinks piled high with pots and pans as everyone is going to the table for a meal. Some things need to soak, but with a little planning and attention, you can sit down for the meal and have the sink still operational. The troublemakers are not only the roasting and sauté pans. There are trickier characters—like the colander or the steamer or even the fluted glasses you brought out to celebrate. They can clog everything up.

They are all easy enough to clean, but you must have water, and you must have room, and you must notice what needs what. All of the pans that did not have contact with fats or oils are your first target. Get the colander done, dry it, and put it away. If you put the fluted champagne glasses in the sink, then there is no way to get anything done. Either stash them to the side for the very end, or quickly get them washed and whisk them off to safety. If you have kept some work-space clear and have access to water, these can all be done in seconds. You must move and be able to move quickly; your place is at the table.

One of the trickiest clogs is the pasta pot with its strainer insert. I do mine at the very end, in case I need to make more pasta for that meal or for the next day. But if the pot has made it into the sink, then you have no choice, you must deal with it. The strainer has to go first; it will be slick with oil and protein. Rinse it well, then clean it inside and out with a very soapy sponge and rinse it well, so the soap does not show up a day later in the pasta.

Until the strainer is clean, do not put anything into the pot. Once the strainer is out of way, then rinse the pasta pot. If you want, you can use it for the hot soapy water.

You will learn to look at a sink full of dishes, pots, and pans and figure out a way to unravel it. If the sink is piled high as you go into dinner, then a traffic jam is a certainty. Make a little plan for your return, some way that you can clear that sink quickly and have it ready for the inevitable new batch of dirty dishes. Many times, I have gone back into the kitchen to prepare the salad or the dessert and used that specific intermission to get the sink clear of other dishes. The diners can wait a moment; it is a good pause, and you can use the time to clear the runway. When the sink is clear, then the pieces returning from dinner can simply be handled as regular traffic.

Tips

Here are a few basic tips to make your dishwashing tasks easier. It is a modest list. Everyone who washes dishes could add their own specifics to it. That is the subtlety of dishwashing.

- Rinse your sponge in cold water when you are all done with it. It will clear the soap but also cool the sponge.

- Two quiet dishwashing secrets are baking soda and salt. They can be used as abrasives, and they also absorb odor and penetrate into cutting boards.

- Before putting rubber gloves on, rub some hand lotion into your hands. The gloves will go on and come off with much more ease.

- A sour sponge or cloth can sour your relation to the task.

- Clean dish towels can be as pleasurable as clean sheets.

- Linen dish towels are easier to clean than cotton ones—their open weave allows them to be more deeply cleaned. It is a difference that becomes clearer in time.

I have many dishwashing memories. Times in the mountains where we waited an hour for the water to boil. Times when we needed a bucket line to handle all the dishes, where spirits were high, and you were lucky to be included. Times when I thought, "How could all these people simply leave after dinner, without realizing how much was yet to be done?"

But no recollection is more precious than that of Peter Cipra, the Seattle chef who ran the famous Seattle restaurant Labuznik until 1999. Cipra was a large, physical man, and he was very intense. Never was that more clear than when he was closing up his restaurant each evening. He had been trained in Czech kitchens, in particular the wealthy health resort hotels. There was no place for error or bacteria.

He cleaned everything—counters, walls, backsplash, sink, hoses, oven doors, racks, vents, towel bars, light fixtures— as well as all of the dishes and equipment. He kept a bucket of soap and water in the center and worked from there. Trays with trays, sauté pans with sauté pans, and all the glassware at once, rinsed and then put into the dishwasher. The tools soaked in another bucket; the knives were way off to the side doing their own soak.

The kitchen was both his operating room and his theater. He butchered all his own meats in the morning and plated all his entrees in the evening. And every evening ended the same way—with perfect, clean counters and an empty, shining sink. That was the tradition and the signal of the end of the workday—the closing was as important and detailed and obvious as the opening.

You could watch—from off to the side—as he stored any extra food or sauce or vegetable. For one, there would be containers that he would force the air out of as he closed the top. For others, plastic wrap would seal the surface. There was a place and method for everything.

I learned a great deal over twenty years, watching Peter Cipra cook. But I learned as much, if not more, watching him clean up.

2

DECISIONS

and Details

———

YOU WILL KNOW YOUR STATE OF MIND when you wash the dishes. Your care or your impatience; your attention or your distraction. You will see yourself, at that moment, clearly. It is not a task that draws a crowd. It is a solitary undertaking. And it has no instructions or even formats.

You might be pleased with the privacy or trapped with the isolation. The dishes may seem to be the ending of a meal or more like the trash behind the bleachers. The task may seem to be an honor or a burden. Whatever the case, you will see it, and you will see how you feel about it.

The dishes are the less-than-romantic truth of a meal—the props left on the stage after a play has ended. They signal the pace, the intricacy, and turmoil of the meal, and the results of its performance. They can be pleasant or horrid, but the actors have moved on, and you have the cleanup. And you will think something of it.

You might feel you have better things to do, or you might imagine you are the best person for such a task, or you might wonder where to begin. Doing the dishes will tell you things. And if someone should join you, it will tell you things about them as well. It is a particular one-act play, with no audience but your own thoughts and some silverware. Curiously, by the time I have finished the dishwashing, I always feel better than when I started. It can be a kind of digestive, to both the food

You will know
your state of mind
when you wash the
dishes. Your care
or your impatience;
your attention
or your distraction.
You will see yourself,
at that moment,
clearly.

served and the emotions of the day. I may approach the dishwashing from different directions, depending on my moods and my passions, but the dishes will always ask, "How would you like to handle us?"

Washing dishes gives you many opportunities to make decisions. How you proceed, how you treat each piece comes out of a momentary analysis. There are plenty of chances when you are doing the dishes to use your head. If you know that the big pot was simply the only thing available to soak the muddy spinach, for example, then you know that cleaning it will be but a moment's task. Here are some guidelines to help.

Protect your dishwater. It has a strength—keep it fresh so it can cut through grease and do its work. Do not let anyone stack it with food-covered plates. For the most part, its task is to provide strong, hot, soapy water for rinsed silverware and the rest of the dishes, pans, and counters.

Make judgments. Nothing can go well if the counter and sink are full of trays and pans. Decide what is what. A sauté pan may need soaking, but it may also only need a quick pass with a sponge to be clean. You must look and judge what things can be cleaned the quickest. What things will need elbow grease. A pan that only needs a quick rinse is, in a way, an advantage—but only if you recognize the advantage.

You cannot do the dishes without discrimination—in the best sense of the word. You will make multiple decisions regarding value, condition, appearance, and performance. If you delay or fail to judge each piece, then you will have made your task much more difficult.

Bowls are a good example. They can come from several places, but oftentimes there will be a stack of different bowls needing to be washed. Some may be holdovers from making the dessert or the salad, soaking the vegetables, or mixing the pasta.

When you see four or five bowls of all shapes, sizes, colors, and uses waiting to be cleaned, you must judge them, rank them, and get them ready anew or get them out. Dish towels know perfectly well how to handle freshly washed bowls. Or you can set the bowls to dry, but not to wash, in the dishwasher. I never want the bowls washed in the machine; they take up too much room. As well, I typically need one of them before the dishwashing cycle is finished.

The plastic bowl for the salad spinner is an interesting character. It has a plastic strainer insert that is best cleaned immediately, before the greens can dry on its surface. If the salad spinner should show up with your dishes, it can, in a way, be helpful. It is not built for the longer-term rigor of dishwashing but in certain cases,

Doing the dishes
will tell you things.
And if someone
should join you,
it will tell you
things about them
as well.

it can be a very good soap bowl. Clear the sink. Clean the strainer, rinse it, and get it put away. Rinse the plastic bowl well, then fill it slowly with soap and hot water. It can now be your main center for the rest of the dishes. And it can always use a good scrubbing.

3

TOOLS, TRICKS,
and Troublemakers

———

SOME THINGS, like whisks, large spatulas, long wooden spoons, or hand colanders will likely be used more than once while cooking a meal. Think of them as a bartender thinks of his cocktail shakers—use them, wash them, dry them, and have them ready for the next task. Nothing is sillier than having a large bowl of dishwater with a whisk and three long spoons in it. It takes but a moment to clean and get them out of there; they should never go in the dishwasher.

FOOD PROCESSORS/FOOD MILLS

You cannot leave food processors to join in the dishes from dinner. They are bulky, demanding, and too awkward to be in that group. If you use them, clean them, right then. You need that corner of the counter free. If I am using it to make pesto, then I am careful to finish the task, completely, before starting to cook. There are few things (the electric mixing bowl being one) that can so intractably take up space as the brilliant blender. Get it put away, so not even the cord is showing. As a rule, when I begin to cook, I expect all of the equipment and dishware that came before will have been cleaned, dried, and put away.

The food processor is an interesting character. It might as well be an operational satellite for all its likeness to the rest of your cooking equipment. It is, in its own way, a carburetor of food, a complicated mixer that must sacrifice simplicity and ease for power and efficiency.

It has necessary corners and crevices that would never be approved on less complex devices, but while it does not clean easily, it does have brilliant talents, and you must give it a special dispensation.

It is discouraging to see a food processor in the dishwasher. It is not a machine that mingles well with others. Its work is very specific and typically done by the time a meal is started. So as you rinse and clean each piece *by hand*, lay it on a surface to drain. When all of the parts are done, grab a medium dish towel and finish the drying. To be fair, it is hard to dry this group well. Reassemble the machine, sliding parts into place, and stack it back onto the motor. Then you can begin dinner prep.

By contrast, an Italian food mill is practically medieval. Mine has literally three parts—the disc, the handle, and the body. It is a wondrous piece of equipment, particularly with cooked beans or tomatoes or soft fruit. Unlike the food processor, the food mill is often needed right in the very belly of cooking, when there is a lot going on.

Still, it can clog up a disproportionate amount of space. I have found it stuck at the bottom of a dish pile, waiting for special attention. Try to clean it right after using it. It has sharp edges, but it is quite easy to dispatch when nothing has dried on its surface. And then, of course, get it put away—rarely does it do double duty during a meal.

PASTA POT

Some things can do a second duty and help with the dishwashing. A good pasta pot, with its strainer, can be a bully for attention. But if you rinse it and refill it with soap, then you can get the strainer cleaned and use the pot for your new base of dishwashing. It can catch up with the strainer and the lid later.

SHARP KNIVES

Never put knives in soapy water; lurking below the bubbles, they will inevitably cut someone, and usually an innocent. Lay them on the counter and wash each one individually. Once you have cleaned them, do not add them to the rack of drying dishes; put them away. Everyone is reaching for something as the dishes pile up, so be sure they do not grab the sharp knife instead of that serving spoon. Funny thing about a knife: it loves to cut. That is all it knows.

SAUTÉ PANS/SHEET PANS

Sauté pans and sheet pans are the main tools of cooking, and they each have particular quirks. Some of the surfaces are coated and cannot be scrubbed. Some are steel and need a good scrubbing. I know cooks that use only a special soap on their cast-iron skillets—and some that use no soap at all. You need to keep the differences sorted.

You may only have a single sink, and it may be small, so your task is to keep it clean and draining well. A frying pan plopped into it is no help unless you are ready to clean that pan. When people clear the table, it is common to see all the silverware floating in greasy water in the dinner's sauté pan. That is when doing the dishes seems like a nightmare.

There is a pan that was used to poach a pear, and there is a pan that was used to brown and caramelize a pork chop. The first will take but a few seconds to clean: rinse, soap, rinse again, and then dry and put away. The second pan will take longer. It may need to soak and then be scrubbed. You must, in a moment's time, always know the difference between the two.

GLASSWARE

I always flinch when someone suggests using the good champagne glasses. For one thing, they usually need a buffing up, having gathered dust. But they also can clog up all the dishwashing runways. If it is time to use them and celebrate, then make a note of how many there are and their condition. If they are fragile or crystal, they will need to be washed by hand.

You must decide: clean them before you start the dishes or set them well aside and do them when there is nothing left in the sink. If you clean them before, make certain there is no cast-iron skillet or pan nearby and make sure the sink is not greasy or they might slip. They need their own flat surface to dry. Use a soft dish towel and stay with them until they are back on their shelves. Or, if someone is helping you with the dishes, put them on the "dry the glasses" detail. You will have more freedom to work if the glasses are in good hands and out of your way.

There is an elegance but also a danger to good glassware. Some of the worst cuts in a kitchen are from the sharp edge of a broken glass. Be very careful if you lay them in soapy warm water. And be even more careful when you are cleaning the inside of a glass—use either a soft brush or your two fingers and a dishcloth within the glass. The danger comes from the circular motion, which might break the edge. If you should break a glass, gather all of the pieces and put them into a box or some other container, so they will not be a danger to someone pushing down on the trash later.

The truth is, you will develop a dishwashing value system for every piece in your kitchen, and eventually in most kitchens. You will know, by sight, the tasks of each piece, its liabilities and its advantages. When a sharp knife comes to the sink, you will mark it for special care. When the coffee pot comes, you will know that coffee shares space poorly—the grounds need their own care and the residue needs extra soap. When the porcelain coffee pot comes, I am always reminded of a coffee pot with a broken beak—porcelain has no defense against cast-iron pans.

There is
an elegance but
also a danger
to good
glassware.

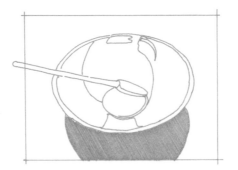

4

Three Recipes

FROM THE DISHES' POINT OF VIEW

IT IS NOT UNCOMMON that some ingredients, and some recipes, are prejudged by the difficulty of their preparation. You may need to wash a fresh head of lettuce from a farm stand three times to clean the leaves. Or you may need three bowls (small, medium, and large) to sauté a fish properly. I rarely consider how many bowls or pans a recipe might need, but I do keep a plan in mind for how to wash them all. And what that might involve. It helps to keep that side of things in general order. It is a little unromantic to think of a recipe from the point of view of washing its dishes. But while you are cooking, keep a few of the details in mind and the joy comes from the end result: a beautiful simple meal that you can enjoy fully, without thinking about what you have to do after.

Four-Egg Omelet

———

This is a straightforward recipe and a lovely one. As the seasons change, add small elements of any new arrivals, like chives and cherry tomatoes, young sprigs of arugula, a couple of fresh wild mushrooms, a tiny piece of an herb, or a spoonful of fresh goat cheese.

The recipe anticipates the dishes and equipment you might need. When you serve the omelet, try to have everything, except the soaking pan, washed. That is the test.

INGREDIENTS

4 eggs

Parsley and perhaps chives

1 tbsp. freshly grated Parmigiano-Reggiano cheese

1 tbsp. cold milk or water

1 fat tbsp. cold butter

Flake salt

Freshly ground pepper

EQUIPMENT

Mixing bowl

Small bowl

10-inch sauté pan

2 plates

Cutting board

Sharp knife

Small cheese grater

Whisk

Rubber spatula

2 forks

2 water glasses

Making an omelet
is a kind of
card trick.
Making an omelet
and having the
dishes done
before you serve
the omelet is
a tricky card trick.

Crack the eggs into the mixing bowl, putting the shells into the smaller bowl or tossing them out. Heat the pan on medium low and put the plates in a slightly warmed oven to take the chill off them.

Chop a few sprigs of parsley and/or the chives and grate a tablespoon of Parmigiano-Reggiano cheese onto the corner of the cutting board. Add the cold water or milk and a pinch each of salt and pepper to the eggs, and then mix with the whisk. The French, who have been studying eggs while others have been sleeping, recommend that you beat the eggs only until they are barely mixed, and lightly at that.

Add the butter to the pan. It should sizzle gently and begin to lose its foam (Note: if the pan is too hot, the butter will start to burn immediately—start over!). Add the eggs, scraping the sides of the bowl with the spatula to get all of the egg. Put the spatula into the smaller bowl.

Swirl the pan to even out the eggs. It must set for a moment, and in that moment, take the mixing bowl and the whisk quickly to the sink, rinsing both, and adding hot water and dish soap to the mixing bowl. As it is slowly filling, clean the whisk, shake it, and put it away.

Back to the eggs. Lift up the outer edges with the spatula and tilt the pan to let some of the unset egg tuck in behind. Add some of the cheese, some of the parsley/chives, and some salt and pepper, and when there is just a little liquid egg left, fold the omelet in half, tilting the pan just a bit. It is done.

You can put the omelet on one of the heated plates or use the spatula to cut it in half and put half on each plate. Sprinkle the rest of the cheese and then the parsley on top.

Quickly rinse the spatula, the small bowl, and the cutting board, wipe them with a soapy sponge or cloth, rinse them again, and set them aside. All in twenty seconds. Bring the pan over, rinse it quickly with hot water, and add some of the soapy water to it and set it aside. Empty and rinse the mixing bowl and leave it to drain.

The sink should be empty. Get the omelet to the table with the plates, the forks, and the glasses. When you return, do the pan first; the soaking will have loosened the egg. Rinse it and dry it and then put the plates into the sink, run some water into them, and let them soak a moment. The egg yolk was the secret to the preservation of paint during the Renaissance—do not let the egg dry; it only gets more stubborn. You can clean the plates, glasses, and forks using the small bowl, a sponge or dish-cloth, and a little soap. Voila! No dirty dishes.

Making an omelet is a kind of card trick. Making an omelet and having the dishes done before you serve the omelet is a tricky card trick.

Fresh Spinach, Sautéed in Olive Oil and Garlic

Spinach, especially in the spring and early summer, is a remarkable vegetable, with a clear and subtle taste. I rarely serve it with anything else. But a pound or two of fresh spinach leaves can take up an entire sink and briefly involve several pots. It must be well-rinsed; the slightest grit left behind is a false note. You will need a large mixing bowl in which to rinse the spinach. It may, for a moment, seem a considerable fuss to make this dish. And the servings, even from two pounds of spinach, are very modest. But that is the brilliance of it, and what makes it worth the effort. It is a flurry of labor and bowls for a lovely moment of tasting.

INGREDIENTS

2 pounds fresh spinach leaves, washed and stemmed

Cold water

Flake salt

1/2 cup extra virgin olive oil

2 garlic cloves, peeled and crushed

Freshly ground pepper

EQUIPMENT

Large mixing bowl

Large colander

Large pot with lid for steaming

Tongs

Small colander

10-inch sauté pan

Rubber spatula

1 dinner plate, warmed

2 small plates, warmed

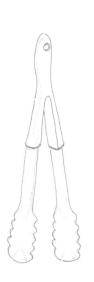

Soak the spinach in plenty of cold water in the largest bowl you have or in a very clean sink. Spinach in the spring means it may have been through rains and thus may be covered in soil, so it may take two or three rinses to get it clean. Each time you rinse, lift out the spinach so the dirt is left behind.

When it is clean, put the spinach, with the water still clinging to it, into a large colander and set it over the bowl or sink. Heat your large pot over medium heat, and the moment it is hot, pour half of the dripping spinach into it. It should sizzle a bit. Wait a moment for it to heat, and then turn over that first batch and add the rest with a good pinch of salt. Cover the pot. The spinach will only need 4 minutes or so to cook, depending on its size and freshness, and you will need to turn the batch with tongs in a minute to be certain it cooks evenly.

For a moment, the sink is free, and you must quickly use the time to rinse and clean the large bowl and the large colander. They are taking up far too much room. Start to fill the large bowl with hot water and soap. As it fills, wash the colander in the soapy water and then rinse it clean. You do not need to fill the large bowl; it is not staying. If you have some stray utensils or dishes nearby, clean them quickly as well. But your first need is to get that big bowl clean and put away. Dump out the soapy water, rinse the bowl, dry it, and then put it and the large colander away.

Turn the spinach. If it seems dry, add a little water
to quickly steam it. It is ready when it has wilted, but
before it becomes mushy. Lift out the spinach with the
tongs—what was once enough to fill a sink will now
be only a small cluster barely enough to cover a dinner
plate. Place the spinach in the smaller colander and
press it a bit to squeeze some of the liquid out.

Rinse the large pot with hot water to clear the spinach
residue and let the small colander rest sitting atop it,
to keep it warm.

Heat the sauté pan on medium or just below and add
enough olive oil to cover the surface. Add the garlic
cloves and let them brown slightly to flavor the oil.
Press one last time on the spinach and add it to the oil
and garlic, gently so there is no splattering. Add a good
pinch of salt and stir the spinach with the spatula to
coat it with the oil.

Have the warmed dinner plate close by. When the
spinach has sautéed for two minutes, lift it out and onto
the dinner plate. Pour the hot garlic oil over the top,
crack some fresh pepper and a bit of salt for the edges.
It can now sit for a moment.

Add hot water and soap to the large pot, cleaning the
small colander and the lid as you do, and the tongs as
well. Bring the sauté pan over, rinse it with hot water

Cooking is
a flurry of labor
and bowls for
a lovely moment
of tasting.

and then quickly clean it with the soapy water. It should not take but a minute for all of this.

The spinach has been carefully tended on the warm dinner plate. Serve it on the warmed smaller plates, with perhaps a touch more olive oil. It is one voice, alone on the stage, but if it is a fresh spinach and good olive oil, everyone will pay attention. The large pot is ready for the few dishes to return.

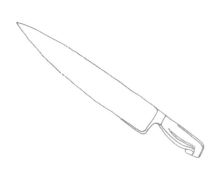

A Fresh Green Salad and
a Simple Vinaigrette Dressing

———

Nothing, of course, is simple, and a simple salad is one
of the more complicated simplicities. Done well, it will
even seem straightforward. It does take some rushing
about and attention, and pans will rattle past each other
for little while, but then it is done. When you serve the
salad, there should be little evidence of the flurry other
than the two plates and the salad bowl itself. All the
other equipment should be cleaned and put away.

As you get comfortable with the basics of making the
salad, you can add variations of greens—each season has
its own variety, even winter. Start with small pieces of
arugula or endive or radicchio. Add more as you learn
what tastes are most favored. The brightness of the
vinegar and the lemon in the dressing will help with any
new greens, even those that are bitter.

INGREDIENTS

1 head bibb or
   red leaf lettuce

1 small shallot, peeled
   and chopped

1 tbsp. red wine vinegar

1 lemon

1 teaspoon French mustard

Flake salt

$1/4$ to $1/2$ cup extra virgin
   olive oil

Freshly ground pepper

EQUIPMENT

2 or 3 large mixing bowls

Cutting board

Chopping knife

Salad spinner

Small glass bowl

Salad bowl

Small whisk or fork

Two dinner or salad plates

Soak your greens in a large pan with fresh cold water.
Soak even the greens that say they are "prewashed."
There must be enough room for all the greens to be
submerged. They can rest in the water for 10 or 15
minutes—in many cases, the soaking will revive them,
especially if they have just been picked. Note that if
they were rained on just before they were picked, you
may need to rinse them two or three times before the
rinse water is clear. You also may need more than one
soaking bowl to keep different varieties of greens separate. The heartier greens can be washed together.
The softer varieties hold their shape best if given space
and some separate attention.

Once the soaking water is totally clear, carefully lift the
greens out, leaving the water behind. Give them a shake

and place them in the salad spinner (or colander). Spin the greens (or roll them in a large dry towel) and keep them cool.

To make the vinaigrette, place the shallot into a glass or ceramic bowl. Add a healthy pinch of sea salt, the red wine vinegar, a squeeze of a lemon, and the French mustard. Stir and let this sit for 30 minutes.

While waiting for the vinaigrette, finish the greens, drying and trimming as needed, then place them in the salad bowl with a damp towel on top. Then clean all of the service bowls. Choose the one that best fits in the sink as your soap bowl and work from there. The other bowls may be greasy from the soaking lettuce; rinse them first, then use ample soap to clean them. Wash the cutting board, so the shallot smell does not sink in or spread where it does not belong. Dry the board and the bowls and put them away, out of sight.

Then clean the salad spinner. It must not be left hanging around, mingling. The spinner is a medieval centrifuge, and there is nothing else quite like it in the kitchen. Even the newest models are awkward and once apart, unwieldy. Use the soap bowl to bring order and get the spinner clean, part by part. With a dry towel, clean the many surfaces of the spinner, put it back together, and then back where it belongs. It takes up too much space if left on the counter.

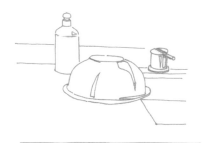

Now you can finish the vinaigrette. Using a fork or small whisk, begin stirring the vinegar mix and slowly add about a 1/4 cup of the olive oil. Stir well and then taste. Add a few drops of cold water to help the dressing emulsify. If the vinegar seems too strong, add a bit more olive oil and check to see if it needs more salt. Crack some fresh black pepper into it.

Add part of the dressing to the salad greens and toss them well with the tongs, or your clean hands. Taste the greens, and if needed, add more of the dressing and toss the greens two or three times. Measure out the salad you need onto the plates, being careful to keep the greens from clumping or losing their freshness. If you are plating all of the greens, then make a note to clean the salad bowl, before anything can be stacked into it.

For a "simple salad," it will have taken four or five bowls to get all the ingredients cleaned, prepped, and in place and some nimble mixing to change the greens from one state to another. The counter may have been covered with equipment, but with some judgment and care along the way, it can be clear as you present the salad plates. The dish towels should be left hanging to dry.

A salad is a thoughtfully prepared composition of fresh, clean ingredients. When the proportions are correct and the greens seem most alive and buoyant, time appears to have slowed for a moment. Your kitchen should have some of that composition as well.

A simple salad
is one of the
more complicated
simplicities.

5

QUIET VILLAINS
and Unexpected Friends

———

WHEN YOU ARE WASHING THE DISHES, you may find yourself having strong reactions to particular pieces, the way people do with other people. Some are "your type"; others, not so much. There is a place for sentiment when doing the dishes. I have used some of my pans and pots for thirty years. I know them. I know their dings, I know their talents, and I can see where they were dropped or mistakenly gouged. They are always the ones to get the best wash, top and bottom.

There are pieces, often glasses, that are irreplaceable. The designer Marc Newson created two styles of drinking glass for the Finnish manufacturer Iittala. They did not sell brilliantly, but they are beloved by whoever was lucky enough to buy them. Iittala, in fact, brought them back into production once, and we bought all that we could before they again went out of stock.

These glasses are the silk of dishes—you never forget them—but they are not easy to wash. They are rounded at the bottom and narrow at the top. The glass is superb but thin, and they certainly do not stack. You must wash each one, by itself, carefully putting two fingers into the glass with a dishcloth and slowly cleaning the interior. (There are tools that are designed to do this. Soft sponges with an attached handle seem to work best). Once they are clean, having interrupted all of the rest of the washing, then you might as well either dry them or turn them to dry on a clean cloth. If you leave them to dry on a cloth, you must perch them along the edge of the cloth to allow a bit of air to circulate and keep them from steaming.

We visit a wonderful couple here on Whidbey Island that have perfected—and babied—their cast-iron pans. You are welcome to cook with the pans, but you will never see them being washed. The pans never face dish soap; they are simply not a part of the procedures at the sink. They are cleaned with salt and towel and a small dab of lard. Their pans, of course, are lovely.

Big Bertha

We have a very large stainless bowl called Big Bertha for washing bags of spinach or for mixing salads for more than two or three people. It fills the sink and in fact does not even sit flat within it, so it is of no use as a center soap bowl. When you have such a thing, you must note that it has come into the sink and that it must be dealt with. The large bowl, useful as it is, can tie up all of the progress and all of the "unfoldings" in the kitchen.

If it has been used for washing spinach, it may be a little greasy and have loose dirt in it, but a quick rinsing with a good, wide sponge will do the job, and a fresh dish towel will make it ready to be stored again. If it has been used to toss a salad, then it is probably coated with a film of olive oil. You must first give it a good rinse with hot water and then wash it again with very soapy water.

You need room to do all of the dishes, and typically the extra-large bowl is there right at the most inconvenient time. Give it your fullest attention, and get it dispatched. Otherwise, it will simply hog space, and soon someone will load it with other dishes, which will, in turn, get covered in the olive oil and the dressing and make your task more difficult and time consuming.

The Mighty Dish Towel

You cannot wash dishes without a clean, dry dish towel—
or better yet, two or three of them and more in a nearby
drawer. A good towel is like a good hat—it needs a place
to rest. I have three or four hooks and bars scattered
around the kitchen, where the towels can dry, out of way,
and still be handy. Honestly, a good towel can make the
whole task make sense. Suddenly, bowls and platters that
would tie up the operation are back where they belong.

You can use terry cloth towels, or linen or cotton or a
blend of the two. Every culture has certain qualities that
they prefer in their dish towels. Whichever type you
prefer must absorb well, dry efficiently, and resist odor,
mildew, and stains. A very good dish towel will last
many years and still look good in a garage sale after you
are gone.

You must wash a dish towel often to keep it free of
bacteria. Years ago, someone was selling towels that were
made for the dining cars on the Finnish railway. They
were brilliant—brightly colored and absorbent and soft.
I wish I still had them.

A good towel is
like a good hat—
it needs a place
to rest.

Dishwasher

Many people have a dishwasher. It was once a great luxury, but now it is a kitchen standard, like electric windows in an automobile. Curiously, many people do not use their machine, at least in the manner it was designed. They will use it as a dish rack or as temporary storage for overflow. I use mine only when we are serving four people or more. For the rest of the time, I use the dishwasher as a holding place for equipment and dishes that have just been washed and will soon be going back to work.

There are many types of dishwashers. Some are quite ingenious, some are economical and environmentally sensitive, and some are a water-and-soap version of a gas guzzler. Like your heating system and your refrigerator, your dishwasher sits somewhere on the spectrum of environmental vs. financial impact. You should learn its strengths and its value.

Whatever your dishwasher type, there are details that you need to take into account. There are loading procedures to maximize cleaning and minimize damage, and the dishwasher itself must be kept clean; the interior edges have no way to clean themselves.

You also must be very careful to keep the screened drain clear. Any broken glass or hard particles will sit there until you carefully remove them. But do so with great caution: I know several people who have been badly cut, reaching into the space.

I rinse everything before it goes in the dishwasher, but some believe that that is one of the tasks and abilities of a dishwasher. There are even certain models that boast of not needing the dishes to be rinsed beforehand. But in truth, your dishwasher does not have a more sophisticated screening system than your own sink. It does not have a built-in disposal. So a little rinsing before the dishes go in will protect the filtering system.

My wife would cheer if she could put the sink into the dishwasher, and the drain and the oven door as well. But I have one imperative regarding the dishwasher: nothing should go into it that is one of a kind—no spatula, no whisk, no mixing bowl, no cake cutter, no kitchen knives, no water pitcher, no carrot peeler, and no oven door. All of these tools and pieces need to be cleaned by hand, dried, and restored to immediate use or put away where they can be found. The dishwasher is for multiples— plates, mugs, everyday glasses, silverware, etc. All the singles must be accounted for, one by one.

There are technical reasons for keeping your knives out of the dishwasher. For one, it is not a recommended method for cleaning steel. Also, most knives have handles that are bolted to their steel frames. The action and heat of the dishwasher is precisely the method you would use to loosen the handles and their fastening screws.

The hot water and then the drying affects the materials and causes them to separate, much as they would with a wooden cutting board if you put it in the machine, and you do not want that.

Counters

It takes some attention to keep your kitchen counters clean and clear. Everything wants to go on them. Bowls and bottles, plates and spoons and lids, pads and glasses, coins and grocery lists, and so forth. Some pieces— the mixer, the coffee machine, the oils, the salt and pepper, the dish soap, the sponges, the hand cleaner, the toaster, the cutting boards—even make claim to permanent residence.

The counters are a bulletin board of things, and all the pieces, quite brilliantly, look like they belong. For most people, the counters are like beaches—some of the time they are covered by a full tide and some of the time they are clearly exposed by a low. But they always have stray bits on them; things that washed in and never quite washed away.

You should clear off the counters as completely and as often as possible. Oil the wood surfaces, scrub the rough surfaces, and clear the smooth ones. And make each piece state, once again, its case for belonging on the counter.

To do the dishes, you need all of the counter space that you can get. You need the space to be clean, and you need it to be available. The sink may be filled with dishes, but nothing can happen and nothing can be ordered if there is no space on the counters.

A dinner plate, sitting on its own, ties up a square foot of a counter. Add a colander, a loaf of bread, and two water glasses, and you can find yourself thinking of ways to avoid using the counter at all. In one sense, it is an unconscious adjustment, like walking around a suitcase without asking, "Why is it right there in the middle of the floor?"

As a cook, you protect the area around your stove. For some reason, there is less protection for the counter area around the sink; even bags of groceries naturally gather and socialize there. Sort it all out, find other holding stations, and keep in mind that you can only get the work done if the counters are clear.

The kitchen counter is not unlike the open screen of a mobile phone—everyone is trying to get on it and have a place, a visible place. The first thing that I notice when visiting another kitchen is how deeply the miscellaneous pieces have asserted claim to the counter. Vitamins, lids, trays, vinegars, stoppers, thermoses, keys, and caps all seem to have intricate arguments for their own importance, position, and reason for being there.

They have their own force, the many things on a counter, and they are ever working and plotting to gently and quietly use all of the available space, filling up the territory.

Vignettes

There is an art to preparing and presenting a meal, and there is an art to putting it all away.

Many times, after a meal or a cleaning frenzy, the counter will become a kind of gallery space. Using dish towels and racks as canvases, forks and knives, lids and glasses, serving spoons and storage jars are laid out in ways that create vignettes. These are moments of honor for the pieces, a kind of roll call—their numbers are matched together in series: lid to lid, body to body, knife to knife. The coffee spoons, which work every day, are momentarily on parade: cleaned, counted, and inspected. The water glasses, which are so often forgotten or skipped, are on their best display, showing their clean and useful form.

It is a time of inventory, but also a time of appreciation and respect. This is the equipment that protects and serves your meals, that makes the task specific and possible. Visit any good restaurant in the hours before they begin their work, and you will find multiple vignettes of equipment, laid out in series. Every kitchen, to some extent, is an operating room, whether conscious of the responsibility or not.

The vignettes make the kitchen counter a gallery until the next meal. The pieces are counted, gathered up, and put away, the towels hung to dry, and the counters themselves scrubbed clean.

There is an art
to preparing and
presenting a meal,
and there is
an art to putting
it all away.

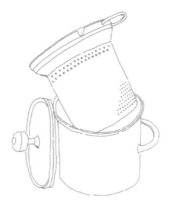

6
Flow

———

IF YOU ARE NOT THERE when the dishes start coming in, then the sink will fill itself entirely. Dirty dishes will be stacked in the dishwater, the utensils wedged in beside. There will be no room to rinse, so no one will rinse.

Beneath the pile may be the oven tray that roasted the vegetables, still covered with olive oil and the bits of onion. A serving platter, laid into the sink unrinsed, can stop an army of dishwashing. Lay two serving spoons across the platter, and no one will even bother to stack on top. Much of dishwashing is perception: if it appears that there can be no progress, then that will be the case.

In a sense, a collection of dirty dishes is a traffic jam. Something caused it; something prevented the different pieces from being able to pass freely, and it is your task to unravel and clear the jam. You are a traffic cop of kitchenware. If there is a backup, then you must find the "villain," the metaphoric flat tire or rear-ender. It may surprise you that just as a traffic jam can be caused by no more than a police car with its lights flashing, so a sink may be stopped cold by four fluted champagne glasses.

Find the source. It may be no more than sheer volume, but more typically, it is bulk and grease and lack of surface area. As you bring order, setting like with like and untangling mixed messes, you will work toward clearing the road—that is, the drain, the dishwater, and the counters. Keep one thing clearly in mind: nothing can proceed until the drain can drain and the dishwater is at full strength. But be careful: often the pile of dishes is an unbalanced glass shanty, and a single misstep or reach can tumble the whole mess, shattering glassware and leaving you with an even worse site.

You must use your head when figuring out this challenge, and that is the best part. For every piece you will ask the following questions: How did it get here? Where has it come from? What was it doing? What does it need? Each piece in the sink has a complaint and would like to speak to someone in charge. That someone is you.

The sink will always tend toward becoming a beaver dam. If there is a great stack-up, carefully get to the bottom of it. Pull out all the pieces, grade and position them based on their needs and condition, and keep an eye out for the easy repairs. If there is simply no sense to be made of it all, then go to true basics. Start by putting like with like: glass with glass, porcelain with porcelain, tray with tray, metal with metal, cast iron with cast iron, bowls with bowls. Get every single thing out of the sink. Then proceed as follows:

Start a large bowl of soapy water but make certain you have room enough around it to rinse. Separate the silverware, rinse it, and add it to the soapy water.

Each piece
in the sink has
a complaint and
would like to
speak to someone
in charge.
That someone
is you.

Rinse the large pans and pots and set them aside. Rinse the plates, top and bottom, away from the soapy water, and stack them. Rinse as well the glasses and set them aside by type. Whisks, tongs, pasta colanders, salad spinners, basters, water pitchers, serving spoons, long spatulas . . . none of these fits into a stack, nor shares space easily. Wash them immediately. Take them all the way to the finish—dried and hanging from hooks or stashed in cupboards. And then your crash site can begin to find some order.

Look for the easiest of the large pots and pans—the ones that were not oiled or buttered or stained. Clean them and get them out of your way. Then move on to the plates and glasses. Now you can tackle the oiled and stained pots and pans with freedom and vigor. At the very end, you should be cleaning the silverware, using fresh soapy water in one large mixing bowl.

DUCK FOR THE HOLIDAYS

I remember my first dishwashing job. I was young and felt quite nimble and could make easy sense of the different pieces to washing restaurant dishes. But one Saturday evening, we served twenty-four duck entrees as a special event. And that left three massive oven trays coated with duck grease. I carried them out into the alley, where we poured off the extra grease into a barrel.

By the time I got back, I had grease up to my proverbial elbows, and on my pants, my sneakers, my shoulder, and all over the counters. I believe that is when I learned all that I now know about dealing with special dishwashing issues. Stop what you are doing and face your foe, right then. Clean and clear the grease, in all its places, or it will spread. And you will be chasing it from one dish to the next.

Three Complications

Typically, there are three complications that tangle up the dishes. The first involves what happened before the meal—what was left on the counter; how the meat or vegetables were prepped, dried, or handled; what cloths and cutting boards were involved. There are issues of health and hazard that are minor unless they are not dealt with, and then they can become dangerous.

For much of the day, a kitchen is used as an open laboratory for more than food. Cleaning chores, plumbing projects, and health care activities can all take place within the space of an afternoon, and the elements of those operations can settle in several directions. They may involve glass cleaner and sponges, wrenches and tape, or used bandages and medicine bottles. Before you can prep or cook, all traces of those other activities need to disappear.

The cutting board and the counters may need a baking soda scrub to ensure that they are clean and sanitary. Check the dish towels for odor or moisture, and do the same for the dishcloth. If they are compromised, they will be no help when needed later. Their earlier tasks—perhaps cleaning something mechanical, patting dry a chicken breast, wiping a spill—may even have left bacteria or odor that would be unhealthy or disastrous to the making of a meal.

You set the table in preparation to serving the meal. Set the counter and the sink, as well, in preparation to making the meal and washing the dishes. Stack three dry dish towels on the counter and check that no mixing bowl has gone astray—hiding in the back of the dishwasher, sitting half-cleaned in the corner, or needing simply to be dried and put away. The bowls will do much of the work, but if left unattended, they will just take up space and look busy.

The second potential complication is the pile of bowls and pans used in food preparation. If they are allowed to hang around, they will complicate the process of getting to the dishes at the end of the meal. Once the food has been washed and soaked and scrubbed and prepped, there is a moment before the actual cooking begins when you must take a place at the sink and quickly rinse, clean, and dry all the bowls and tools that went into preparations. Choose a central bowl for the soap and water and work quickly—the goal is to ensure that any of these pieces could either go right back to work or be put away.

Finally, there is the polite tyranny of certain singular pieces. Each is one of a kind, often oversized, and usually a little awkward. They do not stack or mingle or fit easily. The long barbecue tongs are a good example. Or the V-shaped rack for oven roasting. Or even the gravy boat or the hand-carved salad-mixing tools.

The goal is to
have the process,
like the water,
flow easily.

For each of these, you must make an exception and a notation. They need particular care and until they receive it, they will hold up the entire parade. Even a pair of barbecue tongs soaking in a mixing bowl can stall the process, like a car with a flat tire in traffic. If they are suddenly cleaned and dispatched, then the bowl can go back into action, and we are back on the road.

Because these pieces are awkward in shape or form, they command their own space. By courtesy or expedience, they can sit quietly, acting as if they are like all of the other dishes. Note where they are, and what condition they have gotten themselves into. Then get everything else to pause for a moment and clean those pieces. No good will come from letting them sit around.

The goal is to have the process, like the water, flow easily.

DRAINS

We have a big leaf maple tree, *Acer macrophyllum*, here in the Northwest, with aptly named leaves that can be twelve inches across. When they fall, they pile up and form almost a thatch. There is a city ordinance that each property owner must ensure that the leaves do not back up the sewer drains in the street at the front of their property.

In certain storms, at certain times, the wind and rain will rip a great heft of leaves from the trees. The drains will be completely stopped up by the leaves, and the streets will flood. Until the drains are cleared, everything gets backed up. It may only be four or five leaves, but they are able to completely stop the flow. Their wet, viscous surface will overlap and form a perfect water barrier. All of the incoming rain water, gallons of it, feeding from many directions, will be stalled and over flowed back into the street and onto the sidewalks.

If you go out to the storm drains, you can lift the leaves away and suddenly all of the water will drain and clear, and the crisis will have passed. It is certainly easy enough; the difficulty is more a matter of realizing what is happening and what needs to be done and then getting down into the small center of the jam and clearing the obstruction, letting water flow again.

The drain in the street is not unlike the drain in your sink. They are both crucial and both, for all their simplicity, vulnerable.

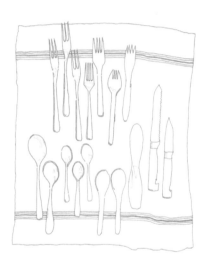

7

THE DAILY
Dishwashing Routine

———

Breakfast

I am typically up first in the morning. There are usually
stray dishes hanging around—a snack plate, a teacup,
a pan still soaking. I use a smaller bowl for dishwashing in the morning. As it fills, I can wash the forks and
stray teaspoons and the wineglass that was hiding in
the other room. Be certain to dispatch any pans from
the night before that need cleaning; they are too heavy
for the details of breakfast and will only sit in the way.
Wash them, dry them, and stash them. You may need to
change the dishwater a couple of times, but keeping
the bowl on call makes doing the breakfast dishes a
simple chore.

Put any pieces drying from the night before away
and empty the dishwasher. Pull out what you need
for breakfast in terms of dishes, glasses, and silverware.
The coffee filter takes but a moment if the dishwater
is already empty and waiting, and people can rinse
out their coffee cups and water glasses, even if they
are rushed.

Lunch

It helps at lunch to know which pan you will use for washing the dishes when the time comes. Sometimes, it may be the salad bowl. If the bowl has dressing in it, or a bit of salad left, then all of the other dishes can do no more than stack up and mingle on the counters. Make a point to get the bowl ready for dishwater and have it filled and freshly soaped before people have finished their lunch. Any cutting boards, colanders, and knives, which are so easily cleaned, should already be put away before the lunch dishes return.

At my work, we have only a service sink, used for many things other than food. As a result, we have become nimble and ingenious at washing the lunch dishes without touching any of the surfaces. This handicap has tightened the parameters for washing and made the dishwater a crucial ally.

Dinner

Early preparation for making dinner typically involves
a negotiation between dishes leftover from the day and
food that needs to be prepped. It is a poor idea to have
a bowl of fresh soapy water in the same sink with fresh
vegetables. It may seem possible to keep them separate
enough to avoid contaminating the vegetables, but it is
an unnecessary constraint and risk.

Clear all of the day's dishes and counters before starting
your preparations for dinner. Wipe and dry the counters.
Rinse out the dishcloth until it has no more soap in it.
You might even rinse the outside of the soap container.
You are done with soap for a moment, and there should
be none of it left to touch your food. You need room—
and you need it to be clean and neutral and dry.

Check that your cutting board(s) is dry, odorless,
and easily reached. The knives as well. If you are
using a dish rack, empty it and check its underside
and interior to ensure that it is not becoming coated
and slick with residue. The dishwasher should be
entirely empty—including the array of lids and empty
jars and plastic containers.

As you begin to prep for dinner, you will generate
pieces that need to be cleaned—bowls and colanders
and such. Do them by hand, when the sink is completely
empty, using only a dishcloth and soap and dry them

immediately. I do not start a bowl of dishwater until all of the prepping has been done. Soap and food are always kept separate.

The counters must also be dry and clear. You need room to cook and once the process has begun, you need to protect that space. Two empty jars, a well-meaning box of chocolates, and the sugar bowl can tie up an entire counter. At some point, you may be laying out warmed plates or cutting the bread, chopping the herbs, or grating the cheese—they will all need free space. It is much easier to make dinner if you have space to work in and are confident that the space is clean.

8

CONCLUSION:

To Wash, To Dry

———

DESPITE ITS DIN AND CLATTER, despite its reputation and its noisy relatives, washing the dishes is in sum an act of grace and rhythm. Ironically, it is often handled and managed almost as an attack—let me at them!—especially by the rush of youth.

But its veterans know the task differently. They know that it is a cast of the hard and the fragile, of the sharp and smooth, of the young and the old. They know that all will be on stage, some in a mad rush, some marked and crusted and slick, some elegant and formal. It is a bustling musical of water and soap, of flow and surface. Done well, the cast-iron shall sit as proudly as the crystal.

Doing the dishes is one of those tasks that you can do in silence or to the full blare of a music system or to your own voice, singing. No one cares, as long as you are the one doing the dishes. I love listening to Astrud Gilberto, Bill Frisell, Richard Strauss, Emmylou Harris, any good Hawaiian guitar player, Rolando Villazón and Anna Netrebko from *La Bohème*, or rock and roll loud enough so you can hear the drums. It is well after the play has ended and the curtain has closed.

Dishwashing can be done as an attack, but that is not what will, in time, maintain the task. It is subtler, gentler, often longer, and more intricate than that. It is the coda to a meal. At times it is quite routine, at times raucous, and at times complex. It is never convenient. The grace is in the handling. You will choose what to favor and what to isolate. Like a barnyard, everyone is clamoring or nosing in and if there are enough dishes, it is hard to see who is who.

Sometimes, of course, you only have a few dishes. And you remember how the meal looked, what you might have changed, why it is important to sit for a minute, how long ago you decided the pasta needed better bowls. You will review the meal—its proportions, its process, its reception. You will note that the broccoli was poorly received. Did you serve too much, was it not fresh, were the plates cold? You will note more than you might recall. You will literally see how the meal performed.

The dishes are the last review.

We went to a birthday party late in the summer—dinner for forty people served at four long tables in a row. And everyone brought something to contribute. By the end, the kitchen was a mess, a mess of many cooks and their broth, pans that could not find a home, pans in pans, and the sink was a vignette of all that could be stuck and wedged into it.

I recruited an ally, gave him five dry dish towels, and told him there were three tasks: load, drip, or dry. We cleared a small table of bags and bottles and glasses, laid a tablecloth on it, and brought it over behind us.

It was Betsy's kitchen. She laughed and said, just leave it, we can do it in the morning. But it was a good time to move about and the dishes were in a riot, and I knew that we could bring some order. It would be a good thank-you present for a lovely meal.

There was not a scrap of space open on the counters, so we put the big roasting pans and the sauté pans on the floor and that opened enough space to empty the sink to the sides. I degreased the sink with one dishcloth until it was clean, washed a great mixing bowl in there and handed it over for "dry and put away," and found a second, smaller bowl to be the center for soap. We washed a dozen tools— spatula, whisk, tongs, serving spoons, knives—in the soap bowl and passed them on to drip dry on the table.

Quickly, we rinsed all the plates and got them loaded into the dishwasher, stashing the silverware in the small bowl with soap. Then we rinsed the various glasses and loaded them, type by type.

We pulled the soap bowl out and bent to the task of first rinsing and then cleaning the sauté pans, top and bottom. They went on the table to dry as well. The roasting pans had been on the outdoor fire—they needed time to soak— so we rinsed them, added more soap, and put them back on the floor.

Soon, one side of the counter was nearly cleared. We got the odds and ends into the dishwasher, wiped the counter clean and then it was ready for the end of the night dishes that would come in from the tables outside.

The dishwasher was full—we added the soaking silverware and got it running. There were still thirty wine goblets to come in, some champagne glasses, and a handful of cups and saucers. They would be sorted on the counter. But it was easy now. There was room, and soap, and clear drains. We had finished our impromptu part of helping with the meal. Somehow, the partnership and the solutions had made some fun out of what appeared at first to be just a mess. By the end, it looked quite sensible.

Washing the
dishes is in sum
an act of grace
and rhythm.

What Can You Get from Washing the Dishes

You probably will not get all you had hoped from washing the dishes, but the doing of it will have a grace and habit that will serve you well. There are some obvious gains, of course. A clean sink and the vignette of the equipment, the glasses, the towels, all in order and space. The end of a meal, the end of an intimacy. The elegance of a matter taken to its finish.

It is like the well-made bed, the neatly folded towel, the clean paint brushes, the weeded and watered and lined garden. It is a statement that carries into the next meal but also into time. The recollection and repetition of task and detail.

Not everyone will be convinced. Someone will still jam a greasy, hot sauté pan right into a cold pile of dishes. Someone else will hide a sharp knife in a pile of suds. Another will set ten wine glasses akimbo in a stock pot. Not everyone will be tempted to *think* about how to wash the dishes. And many will forever think of dishwashing as first cousin to basic manual labor—simply a task of little honor or prestige.

You have, on your side, the distilled forces of order and maintenance. There are some who do the dishes for the clarity and privacy of it, who relish the quiet isolation, and there are some who feel the time and movement is a kind of digestive. Putting things in order, where they belong. In the evening, in particular, there is a peaceful silence when it is all done.

There is a fashion to studying and applying the cooking techniques of different chefs. But there is some truth that a great chef will be as good at cleanup as at the actual cooking. They are both a task and a talent, and they are best done with imagination, attention, and care. They allow each other to succeed. There is no chef who does not have many thoughts and detailed methods for cooking. And there is no chef who does not have many thoughts and detailed methods for cleaning up.

The point of doing the dishes is to complete a task and to put things away. To leave the dishes, pots, pans, tools, and surfaces ready for the next meal. To end one play and to begin another.

You will always have Paris, and there will always be dishes. I will wash, and you can dry.

The dishes
are the
last review.

Acknowledgments

To Sara Bercholz, from Shambhala, who said simply,
"Let us do a book." And that was enough.

I wrote a little piece about washing the dishes and Bruce
Ellison immediately noted, "You have to publish this."
In a way, he is the fuel.

It is the passions that run you—the Canal House girls,
the Cipras, the Stoddards (who washed dishes for me
sixty years ago), the hut boys on Mt. Washington, the
Smiths in Paris, the Walkers and Raffs and Schells on
Whidbey, Sam Betances in Cambridge, Bjorn in Stockholm, Alessandra in Cecina, days at the beach, nights in
cities, sinks and soap and hot water, towels and counters
and racks. The theater of kitchens and food. `

I have always cooked for my family—they are the best
of critics, with an obvious sense that people should eat
together, the food should be good, and the dishes are
simply part of it.

My wife has drawn the illustrations, kept the home,
grown and found and picked and washed and dried all,
from my two children to the cat to the greens to the
flowers to the dish towels. My fortune, the coterie.

About the Author

———

Peter Miller lives with his wife, Colleen, on Whidbey Island, twenty miles north of Seattle. There are many brilliant garden farms, cheesemakers, flower growers, mushrooms, and such tucked in every corner of the Island. They have two children, Joe, a carpenter in Seattle and Nina, an educator with Reach for Change in Stockholm.

During the week, Peter runs an architecture and design bookshop, Peter Miller Books, in a brick-lined alley in Pioneer Square, Seattle. The shop has been open for forty years. He writes, each early morning, in the back room.

Peter is the author of two previous books, *Lunch at the Shop* and *Five Ways to Cook Asparagus*. He hopes to do two more.

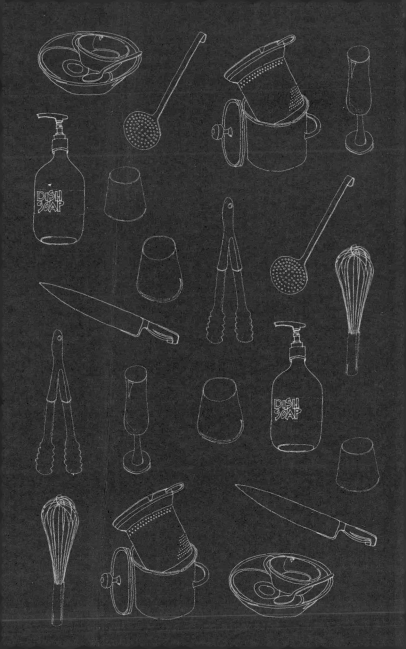